I'm Wearing That!

Story by Jane Clarke
Pictures by David Mostyn

OXFORD
UNIVERSITY PRESS

Yorik the Yellow always wore yellow,

Olaf the Blue always wore blue,

and Erika the Red always wore red.

Then, one day, Mrs Viking went off to build a boat and left Mr Viking in charge.

"Make sure they wear the right colour outfits, dear," she told him. "And don't forget to do the washing!"

"I'll do my best," said Dad.

On Monday, Dad couldn't find one of Erika's red boots.

"Erika," he said, "you will have to wear one of Olaf's spare boots today."

"I'm not wearing that," said Erika. "It's blue. I always wear red. Red is cool. Red is the colour of blood! Blue is the colour of little bluebirds."

4

"Blue is the colour of giant blue whales!" said Dad.

"Cool!" said Erika. She put on the odd blue boot.

On Tuesday, Dad couldn't find Erika's trousers.

"Erika," he said. "You will have to wear a spare pair of Yorik's trousers today."

"I'm not wearing those," said Erika. 'They are yellow. I always wear red. Red is the colour of the sunset! Yellow is the colour of little buttercups."

"Yellow is the colour of pirate gold!" said Dad.

"Gold! That's cool!" said Erika. So she put on Yorik's yellow trousers.

Gold!

On Wednesday, Dad washed Erika's red shirt with Yorik's yellow cloak.

"Wow!" said Dad. "They have both changed colour. The red and the yellow have mixed together."

"Wow!"

"I'm not wearing that shirt," said Erika. "It's orange. Our little kitten is orange."

"Volcanoes are orange!" said Dad.

"Wow! Orange!" said Erika. She put the orange shirt on.

Wow! Orange!

On Wednesday night, Dad left Erika's shield out all night and it went all mouldy and green.

"I'm not wearing that," said Erika on Thursday. "It looks green. Grass is green."
"So is slimy eel soup!" said Dad.
"Cool" said Erika. "Slime green is cool!"
And she put on the green shield.

Cool!

On Friday, Dad washed Erika's red cloak with Olaf's blue trousers.

"Oooooops!" said Dad. "The colours have got mixed up again."

"I'm not wearing that," said Erika. "It's purple, like Mum's old necklace."

"Purple is the colour of a wild and stormy night at sea!" said Dad.

"Cool! Stormy purple!" said Erika, putting on the purple cloak.

On Saturday, Dad boiled the white sheets along with Erika's red helmet.
"Oh dear! Not again!" he groaned.

"I'm not wearing that!" said Erika. "It's pink! Only girls wear pink!"

"You are a girl!" said Dad.

"I'm a Viking," said Erika. "Vikings don't wear pink."

"But pink is the colour of a hungry wolf's tongue!" said Dad.

"That's cool!" said Erika, and she put on the pink helmet.

That's cool!

On Sunday, Mum came home. She gave them all a hug and a kiss.

"Well done dear!" she said to Dad. "Olaf is wearing the right colour... except for his trousers. Yorik is wearing the right colour... except for his cloak, and Erika... is wearing... the right colour... boot."

Well done dear!

I did my best.

"I'll sort it out, dear," said Mum, getting out her hammer and chisel.

"We'll keep the other colours in case we have any more children!" she said, gathering up all the clothes.

She carved the words RED, YELLOW, PINK, GREEN, BLUE, ORANGE and PURPLE on seven different boxes.

Then, on Monday, Mum put out Erika's outfit for her to wear.

"Here you are, Erika."

"I'm not wearing that outfit," said Erika. "All those things are red! I always wear lots of different colours!"

I'm **not** wearing **that** outfit!

Erika opened all the boxes and took out
one green boot,
  one purple boot,
    a pair of pink trousers,
      a red shirt,
        a yellow helmet,

. . . . a blue shield
and an orange cloak.

"But Erika," said Mum. "Your name is Erika the Red!"

"Not any more!" said Erika. She put on her new outfit. "From now on, I'm Erika the Rainbow."

I'm Erica the Rainbow.

Cool!

We want to be Rainbows, too!

And from that day onwards Erika the Rainbow, Yorik the Rainbow and Olaf the Rainbow always wore lots of colours. So life was a whole lot easier for Mr Viking when he was left in charge.

Cool!

Cool!

Cool!

Cool!

Cool!